World Book's Learning Ladders

Inventions

WORLD BOOK

www.worldbook.com

World Book, Inc.
180 North LaSalle Street
Suite 900
Chicago, Illinois 60601
USA

For information about other World Book publications, visit our website at **www.worldbook.com** or call **1-800-WORLDBK (967-5325)**.

For information about sales to schools and libraries, call **1-800-975-3250 (United States); 1-800-837-5365 (Canada)**.

Library of Congress Cataloging-in-Publication Data for this volume has been applied for.

World Book's Learning Ladders
ISBN 978-0-7166-7945-5 (set, hc.)

Inventions
ISBN 978-0-7166-7948-6 (hc.)

Also available as:
ISBN 978-0-7166-7958-5 (e-book)

Printed in China by Shenzhen Wing King Tong Paper Products Co, Ltd., Shenzhen, Guangdong
1st printing December 2017

Staff

Executive Committee
President: Jim O'Rourke
Vice President and Editor in Chief: Paul A. Kobasa
Vice President, Finance: Donald D. Keller
Vice President, Marketing: Jean Lin
Vice President, International Sales: Maksim Rutenberg
Vice President, Technology: Jason Dole
Director, Human Resources: Bev Ecker

Editorial
Director, New Print Publishing: Tom Evans
Senior Editor and Writer: Shawn Brennan
Director, Digital Product Content Development: Emily Kline
Manager, Indexing Services: David Pofelski
Manager, Contracts & Compliance (Rights & Permissions): Loranne K. Shields
Librarian: S. Thomas Richardson

Digital
Director, Digital Product Development: Erika Meller
Digital Product Manager: Jonathan Wills

Graphics and Design
Senior Art Director: Tom Evans
Coordinator, Design Development and Production: Brenda Tropinski
Senior Visual Communications Designer: Melanie J. Bender
Media Researcher: Rosalia Bledsoe

Manufacturing/Pre-Press
Manufacturing Manager: Anne Fritzinger
Proofreader: Nathalie Strassheim

Photographic credits: Cover: © Praetorian Photo/iStockphoto; © Dorling Kindersley/Getty Images: 13; Public Domain: 10; © Shutterstock: 4, 6, 9, 11, 13, 14, 16, 18, 19, 20; U.S. Army: 22; WORLD BOOK photo by Chris Stanley (Museum of Science and Industry, Chicago): 14.

Illustrators: WORLD BOOK illustrations by Quadrum Ltd

What's inside?

An invention is the creation of something new. Some inventions have changed the world and the way we live. This book tells you about some of the inventions you may use every day. You will also learn about some famous and important inventors.

ABC Alphabet

We learn our ABC's when we are very young. We use the alphabet to write our name, read a story, and type on a computer. Each letter stands for a certain sound. Our alphabet developed over thousands of years.

Books help people find information to use and stories to enjoy.

BECKY'S JOURNAL

Before the alphabet, ancient Egyptians wrote with picture symbols called **hieroglyphics** (*HY uhr uh GLYPH ihks*).

It's a fact!

A pangram is a sentence made up to include all the letters of the English alphabet. One example of a pangram is "The quick brown fox jumps over the lazy dog."

There are 26 **letters** in the English alphabet.

We use the alphabet to **read** and **write**.

Glass

Glass is one of the most useful materials in the world. It can be finer than a spider web or stronger than steel. There are many things made of glass that are around us every day.

Look through the glass **window** to see outside.

Glass is made by melting sand and other materials together. Glass may be blown into a bulb shape, squeezed, and stretched.

Eyeglasses help people to see better.

You can see the numbers through the glass face of a **wristwatch**.

It's a fact!

People probably first made glass around 3000 B.C. in Egypt or Mesopotamia (MEHS uh puh TAY mee uh).

A **drinking glass** holds a beverage like water or juice.

Paper

The invention of paper changed the world. We use pens and pencils to write, draw, and color on paper. Schools, businesses, and governments could not work without using paper!

It's a fact!

The kind of paper we use today was invented in China more than 2,000 years ago. Early paper was not used for writing. It was used for wrapping things and making clothing.

Paper is used to write or **draw** on.

Books are printed on paper.

Many people **recycle** paper—they save old paper so it can be made into new paper. Recycled paper saves trees. It can also save energy and help cut down on pollution.

Magazines and **newspapers** are printed on paper.

Elevator

Elevators really give us a lift! They carry people and objects from one floor to another in a building. It would be tiring to climb all the stairs in a skyscraper without an elevator!

American mechanic Elisha Graves Otis invented the safety elevator in 1852. He designed a device that stopped an elevator from falling through the shaft.

The **light** tells us if the elevator is moving up or down through the building.

The elevator **doors** open after the car arrives at the floor.

The passenger pushes a **button** to tell the elevator which floor to stop at.

An elevator hangs on steel cables inside a **shaft** in the building. The elevator works with electricity and is lifted by steel cables up the shaft.

It's a fact!

The ancient Greek mathematician Archimedes (*AHR kuh MEE deez*) invented a type of elevator before 230 B.C. It used ropes and pulleys and could lift one person.

Telephone

We can do so many things with our telephones! Landline telephones let us talk to people. They are connected by wires. Cellular telephones connect us to people from any place in the world. They are wireless—they do not need wires to work. Many cell phones and smartphones let us send text messages, use the internet, and play music, videos, and games! We can even take photos!

This **smartphone** works like a small computer.

We type letters and numbers on the **keyboard** to **text** a friend.

New Message

To Dad

Dad, I went to the library with Henry. I'll be home in 20 minutes.

12

Scottish-born American inventor and teacher Alexander Graham Bell invented the telephone in 1876. In the picture, he is speaking into his invention.

It's a fact!

The word *telephone* comes from two Greek words meaning *far* and *sound*.

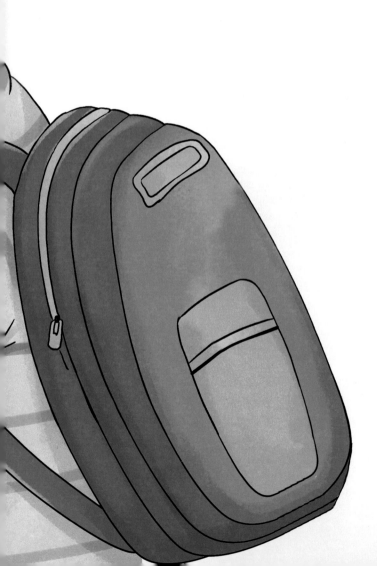

Landline telephones are wired to the building. The wires join up to other wires in a big web. This type of telephone uses wires to connect people to the same call.

Electric light

Without electric light, our world would be a dark place much of the time! Electric power can light up a room or an entire city at night!

A **streetlight** uses electric power to light a street at night.

It's a fact!

Edison's first light bulb lasted 13 ½ hours. Today's energy-efficient light bulbs last up to 15,000 hours.

In 1879, the American inventor Thomas Edison invented the first useful electric **light bulb**.

An electric **lamp** lights up a room.

A **switch** turns the lamp on or off.

15

Bicycle

Riding a bike is faster than walking—and more fun! Bicycles are also good exercise. To ride a bike, you sit on the seat and push the pedals with your feet. All you need is pedal power!

Holding the **handlebars** keeps you steady and helps you steer.

When you squeeze the **brake** on the handlebar, a **brake pad** rubs against the wheel to slow you down.

The Tour de France is a men's bicycle race. It is one of the most popular sporting events in the world.

Always wear a **helmet** to protect your head.

It's a fact!

A tandem bicycle carries two riders, one seated behind the other. Both people pedal the bike forwards.

Two **wheels** spin around and move the bicycle forward.

A bike's **tires** are made of rubber.

Zipper

Zzzzzzzzzip! Zip up your coat—it's time to go outside! A zipper is much faster than buttoning up a coat—and it keeps the cold air out better! What other things do we use zippers for?

Zippers can be used to close or open almost anything. Can you imagine how long it would take you to button up a sleeping bag or tent on a camping trip?

Zippers have two **rows of locking teeth.**

• • • Tugging on a zipper **pull** slides the zipper open and closed.

A **slide** draws the teeth together.

19

 Frozen food

Look at all these frozen foods! Frozen foods stay fresh until we thaw (melt) or cook them. Can you plan a meal from the frozen foods you see in the store?

A **grocery store** sells many types of frozen foods.

Special **packages** help preserve the frozen foods.

Frozen food is cold to the touch!

Frozen **pizza** is fun for dinner.

Ice cream is a popular type of frozen food that we don't need to thaw before we eat it!

Frozen pies make good **desserts**.

It's a fact!

Clarence Birdseye came up with the idea for frozen food in 1915, while he was on a trip in Labrador, Canada. He noticed that quickly frozen fish tasted flavorful and fresh when thawed and cooked.

Computer

Computers are an important part of our everyday lives. Businesses use computers. Students, teachers, and scientists use computers as learning tools. People all over the world use computers to connect to the internet and "talk" to each other. We use computers to play games and watch videos, too!

People carry **laptop** computers with them to use on the go.

The first all-purpose computer was built in 1946. It was so big it filled an entire room!

Some books can be read on a **tablet** computer.

Tap and slide your fingers along the **touch screen** to look at things and move them around.

It's a fact!

The computer mouse got its name because some types have a cord attached to the rear part of the device, which makes it look like a mouse!

Click! A **mouse** moves a pointer along the screen to tell this computer what to do.

Everyday inventions

Think of all the wonderful inventions you use every day in your life. Which inventions do see you in this room?

Words you know

Here are some words that you read earlier in this book. Say them out loud, then try to find the things in the picture.

lamp
glass
computer

book
keyboard
zipper

Which invention would you use to call a friend?

Did you know?

The wheel was invented more than 5,000 years ago. It is one of the oldest and most important inventions.

Sybilla Masters may have been the first female inventor in the American Colonies. Masters invented a corn mill, a machine to crush and grind dried kernels of corn. She became one of the earliest Americans to earn a patent.

A bike invented in 1817 had two wheels and a seat, but no pedals! The rider pushed on the ground with his or her feet to make it move!

The first ice pop was made by accident! In 1905, a boy left a stick in a cup of powdered soda and water outside on a cold night. The next morning, the boy found his drink frozen to the stick! He had to "pop" the frozen treat out of the cup to eat it— and it tasted good!

A patent is a legal document. It says who owns an invention. Thomas A. Edison obtained 1,093 United States patents. That is the most the U.S. Patent Office has ever given to one person!

Josephine Garis Cochrane, an American inventor, patented the first practical mechanical dishwasher.

Puzzles

Word jumble!

We've taken words from the book and mixed up the letters. Can you unscramble the letters to identify the words?

1. cliybec

2. treelticiyc

3. pizrep

4. tablepha

5. reppa

6. lasgs

Answers on page 32.

Double trouble!

These two pictures are not exactly the same. Can you find the five things that are different in picture b?

a

b

28

Match up!

Match the word or words on the left with its picture on the right.

a

1. computer

b

2. bicycle

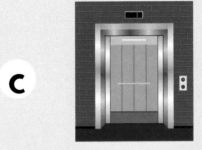
c

3. zipper

d

4. frozen food

e

5. elevator

6. telephone

f

Answers on page 32.

True or false

Can you figure out which of these statements are true? Go to the page numbers given to help you find the answers.

3 The kind of paper we use today was invented in China. **Go to page 8.**

1 There are 25 letters in the English alphabet. **Go to page 5.**

4 Thomas Edison invented the telephone. **Go to page 14.**

5 Alexander Graham Bell invented the bicycle. **Go to page 13.**

2 Glass is made by melting sand and other materials together. **Go to page 6.**

Answers on page 32.

Find out more

Books

125 Cool Inventions by Crispin Boyer and others (National Geographic Children's Books, 2015)
Read about all sorts of fascinating and unusual inventions, from an inflatable bike helmet to a doughnut-dunking machine.

Genius! The Most Astonishing Inventions of All Time by Deborah Kespert (Thames & Hudson, 2015)
Such milestone inventions as the light bulb and the telephone are covered here, along with stories about the person who created them.

Mistakes That Worked by Charlotte Foltz Jones (Delacorte Books for Young Readers, 2016)
Find out how such familiar inventions as cheese and piggy banks were "discovered" by someone making a mistake.

The Way Things Work Now by David Macaulay (HMH Books for Young Readers, revised edition, 2016)
Hybrid cars and e-readers are two of the modern inventions that you can see and read about in this book, along with such classic inventions as the piano.

Websites

Invention Stories
http://invention.si.edu/explore/invention-stories/
From the Smithsonian's National Museum of American History come the stories of people who invented things, from toys to solar panels.

National Gallery for America's Young Inventors
http://www.nmoe.org/gallery/ngind.html
The National Museum of Education hosts this online gallery of young inventors from kindergarten through grade 12. Each year up to six students are inducted.

Scientists and Inventors
https://kids.usa.gov/science/scientists/index.shtml
This U.S. government website contains stories about such inventors as Thomas Edison and the Wright Brothers.

United States Patent and Trademark Office
https://www.uspto.gov/kids/index.html
A special area for kids and teens presents stories about inventors and their patents and includes videos and such activities as coloring pages.

Answers

Puzzles
from pages 28 and 29

Word jumble!
1. bicycle
2. electricity
3. zipper
4. alphabet
5. paper
6. glass

Double trouble!
In picture b, there are two green books on the shelf, the z in the alphabet is backwards, there is less water in the glass, the apple is red, and the stitching on the boy's pants is gone.

Match up!
1. b   2. f   3. a
4. d   5. c   6. e

True or false
from page 30

1. false
2. true
3. true
4. false
5. false

Index